Night Shift

Jonathan Totman was born in Sussex and now lives in Oxfordshire. His pamphlet, *Explosives Licence,* was joint winner of the 2018 iOTA Shot Award and was published by Templar Poetry the same year. Jonathan is a former Fenland Poet Laureate and co-edited poetry magazine *The Fenland Reed* for several years. This is his first full collection.

Night Shift

Jonathan Totman

Pindrop Press

Published 2020 by
Pindrop Press
1 Oakwood Drive
Newton Mearns
Glasgow G77 5PU
UK

www.pindroppress.com

Copyright © Jonathan Totman, 2020

ISBN 978-1-9993559-8-2

Jonathan Totman hereby asserts his moral right to be identified as the author of this book in accordance with the Copyright, Designs and Patents Act of 1988. All rights reserved.

A catalogue record for this book is available from the British Library.

Typeset by Pindrop Press (Palatino Linotype).

Cover image 'The Balance of Dark Over Light', dry point etching, Mike England: www.mikeengland.co.uk

Acknowledgements

Thank you to the editors of the following magazines, anthologies and websites, in which some of these poems, or versions of them, were previously published: *Atrium, Best New British and Irish Poets 2018* (Eyewear Publishing), *Brittle Star, Envoi, The Fenland Poetry Journal, Finished Creatures, The Frogmore Papers, Herrings* (Blue Door Press), *Lighthouse, Orbis, Snakeskin*.

The following poems in this collection, or versions of them, were also published in a pamphlet, *Explosives Licence* (Templar Poetry, 2018): *Explosives Licence; Mushroom Season; Expecting; Stream; Night Shift; Trypophobia; Fireworks; Sky Lantern; Detectorists; Palace Pier; Afterwards, climb; Therapy*. Thank you to Alex McMillen, Managing Editor of Templar, for permission to reprint them here.

I would like to thank the poets and friends whose feedback helped to shape many of these poems: members of Highgate Poets, especially Anne Ballard, Sal Consoli, Norbert Hirschhorn, Frances Galleymore, Mary Hastilow and Paul Stephenson for helpful and inspiring email exchanges; Elisabeth Sennitt Clough, Sarah Mnatzaganian and other members of CB6 Stanza; Heidi Williamson and Rebecca Goss.

I am enormously grateful to Elaine Ewart, Leanne Moden and Poppy Kleiser for the opportunities afforded by the Fenland Poet Laureate scheme.

Thank you to Sharon Black for her careful editorial guidance, for trusting in these poems and for bringing this book into being.

Thanks beyond measure to Mary, my companion in life, and to my mum. With love to my children, Kira and Soren, to Poppy, Rob and Susannah, and remembering my dad. This book is dedicated to all of you.

Contents

15	Marcescent
16	Incompleteness Theorem
17	Who
18	Explosives Licence
19	Power Cut
20	Horse Chestnut
21	Mushroom Season
22	Apology
25	Expecting
26	The Levels
27	Stream
28	Lifeline
29	Tongue-Tied
30	Polar
31	Night Shift
32	Perched
33	The Farmer
37	Sett
38	Trypophobia
39	Owled
40	Arrangements
41	Being a Bonfire
42	Mist
43	Fireworks
44	Sky Lantern
47	Detectorists
48	Palace Pier
49	Slow Puncture
50	Stitch
52	Afterwards, climb
53	Foraging
54	Therapy
55	Tending the Garden

57	The Magic Ingredient
58	Fireworks Again
61	Maple
62	Don't be lulled
63	Ritual
64	Blackberries
65	Where?
66	Seal
67	Switch
68	Energy Performance Gap
69	The Jittery Light
70	'Snow'
71	The Damage
75	Lichen
76	Strike
77	Snake Song
78	Pod
79	Spring, 2020
80	Pencil Sketch
81	Prayer
82	House on Stilts
83	Aubade with Bump
84	All Well
85	Towers

Marcescent

Marcescent: (of a leaf or frond) withering but remaining attached to the stem.
 – Oxford English Dictionary

Hold on to a twigful of leaves.
        Let them flare silverbrown,
    staining the gloom.
            Let them be missed
in the downturned eyes of autumn.

      Hold on,
through winter's tilt and hang.
          As Christmas dangles,
   let them curl and crisp,
       frost to jewellery.

Come spring, come fluke of light,
    let them go,
        strange as old diary pages,
     falling among
crocuses, sweet wrappers, bulging roots.

Incompleteness Theorem

If the world is rationally constructed and has meaning, then there must be such a thing [as an afterlife]. For what sense would there be in creating a being (man), which has such a wide realm of possibilities for its own development and for relationships to others, and then not allowing it to realize even a thousandth of those?
— Kurt Gödel

Picking at moules marinière, you tell me *yes*
you are a scientist, *yes* you go by logic and law
but Dawkins et al. are stuck in a tired old debate
which only goes so far. When you can't swallow,
I think it's because you're talking too fast,
because you're chewing this nugget of thought
about Wittgenstein and the problem of
consciousness and how there might be something
in Gödel that speaks to the notion that life and death
are mathematical mysteries; that you've got this
headful of ideas and it's all you can do to keep
them from slipping out of mind, but you daren't
crack open every shell, daren't look hard at the meat.

Who

And then that pause-in-the-wind moment
when his notes fall out
of the background music of sky,

a rattled coo, toy-like, close
and shapeless on the walk home,
the thought of a feathered warmth,

musty with chick and pellet, the kill
waiting to happen on some dark edge
of field, the thought of other

owls on other nights,
and what you never quite see,
a sense of size, of story,

a faith in what a parent said
taking off into the woods
in the fledgling light.

Explosives Licence

*Is there anything you want to ask me
before we go in?* I laugh
as you unlock the three locks

to the shed, my ten-year-old hands
sliding to coat pockets
for matches I know aren't there.

Inside, your industrial flashlight
flits over cardboard boxes:
Kimbolton Fireworks.

Racks of mortar tubes,
gaffer tape, hard hats,
brown paper-wrapped shells.

I stand still as you rifle.
Sandstorm, Star Mine.
Twist of quick-fuse at my feet.

I've seen you on show night:
nervy, quiet, ducking under
yellow tape in a high-vis jacket,

fading to a figure with a spark.
Later, you show me how to fuse up
rockets at the dining room table,

head bent over a soldering iron.
*Peony, Tiger Willow,
Hummingbird, Roman Candle.*

Power Cut

Candles make an altar of the dining room table.
You've popped out
for kindling, and I lean in
to the pooling wax of my thoughts,
the thrill and bother of a night lifted straight
from Dickens. I don't know it yet
but I'm on fire.
The sleeve of my Adidas top has caught,
and in a moment I'll
feel it, not pain
but a creeping warmth, a sense of something
way too close; in a second I'll turn
to that flame as high as my head,
but right now it's the candles, the prayer-deep dark.

Horse Chestnut

We built our cottage
from leaves and scattered light.
Hollowed out rooms

in the scrub: moss carpets,
nobbled roots for furniture,
canopy as good as any thatching.

Hours disappeared as we
embellished our prickly hideout,
fixed lookout points, escape routes,

days even, as we tunneled
into the copse, stockpiling conkers.
Once, a whole summer went by

before we emerged,
long-haired and chiseled,
scurrying back to the tangled edge

of the lawn, bare soles curling
round pinecones and beechnuts,
past the log stack, rope swing,

skirting the long grass and in,
up, down and around
a house so changed we had to

hunt, had to shout for you:
a yellow glow from a door,
the hint of polished wood.

Mushroom Season

Three days of rain.
A hidden kingdom of spores
fleshes out like tumours.

The shadows
on my father's face.
His new fedora.

There will be ceps,
maybe, chanterelles.
You never know for sure.

*

In the chapel of rest,
wood is lined, cushioned.
I can't stop noticing the cold.

Without the puff
of blood and breath,
skin sinks to the bone.

I don't manage
soft words, soft silence,
the clean tread of grief.

*

Already, the ceps have gone
to slippery leather –
their stems full of holes.

Walk with me Dad,
look after the knife.
Push through

ferns and beech trees,
hold up
the barbed-wire fence.

Apology

Why are you all looking at me
like I'm a lobster in a tank?
So as you scuttle away,

loose to the drift of a tide on the turn,
I consider the lobster,
all tail and claw,

its seabed speckled shell
folding like armour
and the pale softness

beneath those skimpy legs.
Think of its beads of eyes,
its great long whiskers

headlighting the way, and remember too
how the holiday had to have one:
a bin bag on the back seat

pregnant with dazed and doomed crustacean,
taped pincers stabbing at plastic
like some terrible birth

then left to dull in the fridge,
blue blood slowing
as we washed the sand from our toes.

Forgive me, Dad.
If there was cover here,
I'd be straight for the weeds.

* * *

Expecting

Crouching to inspect the sweet peas –
tendrils coiled round wandering stems,
purple flowers like crinkled summer skirts,
laden with dew – I spy, behind the blue
ceramic pot, some stray, domestic tangle:
a pair of maternity tights, gusted from the line,
leaf-light and ghostly, stretched with a memory of body.
I bundle them in a palm and think of
that little life, flexing its shoots of limb:
all those clothes to be worn, the picking up to come.

The Levels

The levels aren't quite as we'd like.
We google hormones on our phones.
Try not to worry; we'll keep an eye.

We get to know the dim blue light,
the click and drag along the bone.
The growth is just as we'd like

we're told, and we study the lines
of graphs, the careful tone
of doctors who must keep an eye.

In my wallet, a fuzzy black and white
picture: minus six months-old.
We haven't found a name we like.

The weeks roll on and still it's fine,
(it's fine unless you think it's not). *No
need to worry, but keep an eye.*

You lie awake for kicks, the signs
give little sign. Our swollen
hearts beat faster than we'd like.
We scan the dark behind our eyes.

Stream

And sometimes – sifting through
tiny clothes, shades of pink and blue and unknown
initials penned on the labels,

or walking now in this patch of wood – my mind curves
back to some recklessness of boyhood:
bare soles on wet moss, the catch of flame.

We wind our way in,
the last bluebells pink in their fading,
leaves lying flat as ribbons unstrung;

a litter of light through the trees
like constellations worked loose,
blinking in the sway of oak and ash;

and a steep-banked stream, slowly reclaiming
the rocks and silt of the latest dam,
water finding its way, like sadness, or like love.

Lifeline

The wave of you
              breaks and she's
    crying for the air
inside her   the light
              crashing through
    the slits of her eyes   rooting
for the milk
              you've readied   you
    who've been mother
for months   lying
              now in the backwash
    of your pain
a nurse at work
              on your torn muscle
    you who've been river
raft   jacket and rope
              who reaches for my hand
    as I'm guided to my
token task   the cut
              no cut to her
    whose vessel is dashed on the rocks
nor you
              the storm that sunk it
    the ground
to which she clings.

Tongue-Tied

Again, you prop yourself up,
tuck her into the nook
of your folded body, guide her
bobbing head to your breast and
wince as she dips and pecks
then tugs herself loose; again
as she arches to a wail, crumpled
face buried in your dress, you
flip her round, manoeuvre her
into the recommended hold,
refusing my worried gaze,
my guessing at the mils she took
from the ten, twenty seconds
counted under your held breath.

Polar

Today it's me who waddles.
She's big for the sling but in
this cold we pull her tight.
You walk ahead so she'll settle.

In the winter garden, lights
are being strung. An aurora
is planned for the evening.
Plastic snow glitters on the fence.

They take it in turns, emperors,
cross frozen sea to stuff
the larders of their stomachs
with fish and squid. Sometimes

I long for days of egg-keeping.
I would wait out blizzards,
balance her life on my feet,
huddle together with the men.

Night Shift

I scoop her, milk-drunk,
sleep-heavy to my shoulder.
Gentle rocking has become the new still.

And in the night's cradle-hold,
the room's alien darknesses,
I make out the sound, downstairs,

of a father. Woken, perhaps,
by a raging throat, or chasing
some feverish thought,

he pads across the floorboards.
Another log for the fire.
Another cork eased out.

She stirs – a tiny whine.
Let me wait a little longer.
Outside, already, blackbirds.

Perched

              this morning
on the branch of my arm
    feathery hair
                   against my cheek
you spot birds   leaf-like
in the winter hedge
               gaze hopping
from twig
        to twig
                to passing car

how we take to the air
    my daughter
at every jab of alarm

you reach for the glass
    its cold transparency startles

    a ghost creature
         flaps and chirps
out there in the frost

The Farmer

Chances are he never showed, or cared,
but as we scurried into gaps between the bales,
dropped down hay chimneys and
crouched in the prickly dark, our hearts
thudding like boots, we'd see him
peering through slits in the corrugated iron,
hear you lure him into conversation,
the stifling quiet before your call:
all clear.
Mouse-like, we'd emerge,
scramble across the stacks, our limbs
well-versed in their architecture,
down a giant's staircase
and under the gate
to you, our lookout, our accomplice.

Years later, and I've trespassed
into fatherhood: this fortress of yours,
this rickety barn.
Crawling now, off through the open door of summer,
your granddaughter roams,
coats herself in cut dry grass,
the smell of old dry grass.
Are you watching, Dad? Is the coast clear?

* * *

Sett

In the car's close warmth,
the long tunnel of the night,
a memory surfaces:

glimpse of fur and motion,
grey hind too low and large for anything
domestic, caught in the headlights as we

bumped down the drive.
Curled in the back and half asleep, I saw
the arrow of him

spin towards earth,
the safety of a hole
and the knowledge of having strayed too far.

He'll be long gone now.
His chamber sealed,
the complex passed to his offspring's offspring.

New entrances, perhaps, new passages
ending in moss and the scent of a mate;
a tumble of cubs deep at the heart.

And I'm gone too.
Driving my own clan down different routes;
the black and white road

and the grey, grey panic at the verge.

Trypophobia

If there is darkness,
give it to me

clean and whole.
Make it sheer

and treacle-thick,
let me sink

without touching the sides.
Forget blips

and bad days,
hang mistakes like

beads round my neck.
Let my rotten

teeth fall out. Tell me straight
where it hurts.

Ferret out
the needling heart,

give me hide
in place of this sieve-like skin.

O give me glass
and aluminium,

make my sentences
unbroken and let us be done

Trypophobia: fear of small holes

Owled

He has found a roost in me.
Claimed a high-up hole,
a radius of undisturbed sky.

He has mapped out his orbit,
his beat. Made it known
he is ready to sink

his talons into any prowler's eyes.
He has trained me to
his rhythms – a ruffling of feathers

at dusk, that stretched elastic sense
of how long he's been gone.
Mornings, I feel for

the silk and down of him.
I turn to the woods.
I listen for his scream.

Arrangements

for Poppy

i.

They arrive in cellophane,
on the fronts of cards. White

as the January sky.
These fitting,

carefully chosen bouquets – what they ask
of our seedling grief.

So visible now,
so unambiguously father.

ii.

We go in, and it's like
fast-forward: the calm ceremony,

the perfume and cut-
stem smell. Vase after vase,

fireworking.
You've hardly spoken since

and here in this little shop
you choose a wild spray,

bursting orange.
We spell our names for the card.

Being a Bonfire

The drill is to gauge the warmth and adjust your distance accordingly. Keep clear of children and dogs and get as far as you can from gas. A ring of stones makes a good container; better yet, a pit. Shoo hedgehogs away. Watch out for stray sparks. Have a bucket of water on standby. Bear in mind that your structure is precarious. Advise minders to wear gloves when handling your ash.

Mist

We watch him: knelt
at the fireplace, scrunching newspaper,
faithful to his gods
of smoke and music, wine
trickling to the roots
of imagination. How he scrapes
the grate, the metal bucket
that seems always full of ash,
a warm grey mist
that makes straight for the throat.

*

We decide on the field behind his house.
Stubble scuffs
our six feet, hugging
the border where rows peter out
to a spot we don't know how we'll know.
When we scatter him
in the hedgerow, it's like
pouring mist
on mist,
like the urn will never empty.

*

Summer, and another year's growth
makes highways for rabbits, rats.
Spent cartridges litter the verge
and pheasants explode
from the barley,
inches from the feet of children
who stand stunned
at the percussion of their flight.
Across the field, a combine-harvester
churns up clouds of dust.

Fireworks

We scatter like sparks on the grass:
torches, cameras, glow-sticks, phones,
all the private lanterns of the heart
drawing their crazy patterns in the dark.
Tubes rigged in rows, loaded with shells,
fuse wire branched like nerve ends.
Smoke on a stage of skies.

Not bad for garden fireworks, he would have said.
The willows of course, and some interesting bouquets,
but the rest is standard stock:
candles, cakes, badly timed flares.
Little thought to theatrics and the finale
is really just a case of throwing up everything that's left
and hoping for the best.

Sky Lantern

In the end
it's just the one.

A fumbling
four-person effort:

torches, matches,
un-gloved hands,

rice paper shell
crinkling and ballooning,

no wind
and then too much.

By the time it's lit,
people have stopped watching.

Numb fingers
hold the structure

from the flame,
wait as the air

warms in its envelope,
a little tug

to say this thing will fly.

* * *

Detectorists

After the BBC series

Ring-pull, battery, penny, wire: earth's return
for the ache in their feet, the dirt between their nails,
a tone they carry in their head like tinnitus.

No test of their faith, mind; they are practiced in patience,
and the light this evening is like Saxon gold.
See them kneeling once more. Primed for the clink

of trowel on metal. Fellow warriors, old wounds
playing up; fellow mourners, laying gifts in the grave.
This time, this time, I can feel it in my bones.

Palace Pier

Like memory, the pull
       of its patched-up walkway:
music, stubbornly cheerful,
       a grey slab of sea
glimpsed between slats,
       the helter-skelter
thought of collapse,
       the almost-never-quite
of the 2p machine
       and the slippery march
beyond the glitz and rattle
       to that gap between rides,
coat flapping madly
       like some great flightless gull.

Slow Puncture

I've not been good to you, old friend.
Listen to the squeaky rattle of your chain,
the animal whine of your brakes. Listen
to your gears clicking and crunching like bones.

Come, let's get grease on those joints.
Let me clean the smog from your spokes.
What tools we have, I'll try. If nothing else,
some air – remember how it was to glide?

Stitch

It's as if you've seen too much:
a hole in your eye
for what can be released.

Wind bullies the last of the leaves,
whips up tears.
Stitches rub in the night.

    *

There were quilts for each of us.
Sewn in the gaps
between the dropping off

and the picking up,
old torn clothes
grafted in for the colour.

    *

They're happy, you say.
So far so good.
I probe for the facts:

pressure and vision.
The light here, Mum –
you can almost feel it.

    *

Rucked up on the bed,
geometry askew,
the latest is family-sized.

Made to be used.
Smells of sleep, milk,
lines of thread like dot-to-dots.

*

Winter looms
and you lift the lid
of your fabric box.

Leaves pile up, like offcuts.
The woods wait
to be re-embroidered.

Afterwards, climb

up here
past the dew pond, the sheep
half hidden beneath Queen Anne's lace,
along the chalk pit ridge
(hear the rooks in their bowl of mist)
and dip down out of the wind.
And though you see the damage:
the fallen branches,
the light let in,
the muddy pools along the path;
though it has you
wading through ferns,
ducking under
the trunks' diagonals,
still this slope of wood
offers up its rough shelter,
baring its sap and heart.

Foraging

for Susannah

Too late for this one –
a cracked egg mess
of fruiting flesh – but there

is that wood-sweet smell,
that fox-rank whiff;
there by your trainer,

a scattering of little unknowns,
come up in the night
like a pod of whales;

there is that drop of milk
on the gills, that Saturn-like ring
around the stem;

there, that spot
where the sweet tooths grow
in the vaulted ferns;

there is your bag
and your dog-eared guide,
the moss and mulch

and the teeming underground –
its root-chatter,
its forest cortex.

Therapy

Week after week
coming back to this
   upstairs room
a paper lampshade's
    yellow glow
familiar tear
  on the arm
    of a brown chair
the bookshelf's promise
     the city's
  noisy indifference
and this quiet
  unquiet exchange
more grit than balm
   more slip and scrape
    a kind
   of slow
     motion
  falling

Tending the Garden

Like blackbirds we bob
            in and out
                      of each other's sight
    as we sift and turn

        not gardening so much
              as discovering
what already lives here   sown
        by design
              or neglect

    crocus cups on tubular stems

        daffodils peeping out of papery hoods

      a silver birch
sliced and stacked
    under flaking tarpaulin
          logs still looped with rope

    the bones of a bird
        heaped like a toy model
     which I buried

then re-buried deeper

          rusty wire   broken glass

  a rickety fence
      overcome with brambles

you're still pottering in a bed
    trying to decide
        what's weed what's not
  gloves long since abandoned

              I watch you pull free
                a knot of roots

        shake off clumps of soil
                        shield your eyes as it scatters

you stand   flushed
  we could let this corner grow a little bit wild.

The Magic Ingredient

for Mum

Dawn peeling back, and already
the soup is on, the scones
defrosting for breakfast.

It's the usual recipe, you say,
when I ask how you get that
gold and crumbling rise.

And I am thinking about salt
and bicarbonate of soda,
and you are thinking about love.

Fireworks again

and there –
that lonely light
blazing its fierce path, rising
to the slow second when it might just
plummet back to earth.

I would give up this grief for you.
I would lift my face with yours
to the painted dark,
the gold and hanging smoke.

* * *

Maple

In the long, ripe days before,
when the waiting roots us
to our turf, we plant a sapling,
ease it into the heavy pot,
upend compost, throw in
handfuls of fertiliser, like ash.

A year on, red leaves cower,
small hands bunching to fists.
Skeleton now, but we can't
bring ourselves to chuck it.
She coasts around the rim,
grabs at soil: yielding, edible.

Don't be lulled

                by aeroplane imitations

    feel first

                    poke

split open the skin

        throw your arms   and legs into it

            your dugadugada

        your curious frown

and roll   each   nugget

      round the lab of your mouth

            note the warmth

    or chill

          the give   the chew

then spit

                  fling

let the debris pile up on the floor

          but look again

                  look

    take it

        this bowl of raspberries

put your two hands in and squeeze

Ritual

Need more, you say,
as we slosh our way
back and forth across the crazy paving,

seeing to our family of pots,
new shoots reaching like language
from their open mouths.

You're right, they're thirsty,
water trickling
through fine compost,

leaking from hidden holes,
the woodlouse caves at the base.
It's the muck they hang on to:

cat shit, petals,
our too-tough bits of veg
blended up by the worms.

Daily, this ritual:
the three-handed hoist of the can,
the spray bouncing off your hand,

compelled to touch,
the pooling at your feet
and the going back for more.

Blackberries

Da! Your whole-body point
steers us off the path, you wobbling
on your new shoulder perch. A bumper year,
the fields edged with trailing stems,
green nuggets bleeding red, then black.
There is still warmth out, and the brambles
are sweet and fairy-tale thick. I lean in, pass up
little fruits, one at a time, plum-sized
in your palm. Never mind the scratches,
the tottering poise – along these wild verges
we are a winged, beaked, purple-faced creature,
popping in berry after berry,
flying further and further from home.

Where?

Each morning I leave,
each bath-time I'm still not back.

And now, not being there
is being on a train:

a great rattling elsewhere,
busy with feet and faces.

Let it be like that.
Think of us as passengers, my love,

when we go: the hush and riot
of carriage, a blur of track

and all those creatures
we rush too quickly past to name.

Seal

We scuttle over wet sand,
point and point at the dark
blob of its head, will her to see

a flash of dog snout,
big baby eyes, something
of its unlikely bulk. A ripple,

a shadow under the surface
of her face – signs slip fast
and we've looked

enough at the open sea.
Waves pull at our ankles
as she dives

to the ground, resumes
her conversation
with the outgoing tide.

Switch

The year folds like a map in a pocket,
its well-walked routes trodden into
the body's circuitry, might-have-beens left
as fallen branches to moss-creep and rot.

How closely she looks. How she stoops
to this leaf, that winter berry,
the hollowed-out spaces
where nourishment comes beetle-dark,

undisturbed. We carry ourselves across
the winter meadow. Quiet
but for the raised voice of the river,
the current of her thoughts

sweeping us back from our slippery resolutions,
the small absences we grant each other,
ourselves. Do look, little one – and yes,
be startled. Show us. The bite of frost

on the step of the stile. The sight, as we turn,
heads bowed against the low sun,
of the grass strung with spider thread,
its wet glint like left-on Christmas lights.

Energy Performance Gap

It's the gap, you explain,
between the blueprint

and the bricks: heat escapes
at the joints. You squeeze in

another hour. Feed.
Time is measured like formula.

At your desk, a shifting architecture
of light. The warmth of

winter sun through glass.
Her cry blows in,

rattles you like a loose door.
You sit at the threshold

of a future home.
It's the noise in the system,

how the rain finds a way.
We wipe out tiny forests of mould.

Nights, you lie awake,
your models cooking up figures,

your spreadsheets glowing red.

The Jittery Light

It's stopped now, that scream,
empty of voice,
that gut-deep swell, breaking

on the rock of my shoulder.
It's stopped, and sleep circles
like a gull around a tourist.

Outside, a bulb in the porch of the church
flicks on and off,
sparked by some movement we can't see,

or broken. The play of it has her:
the yes-no wait,
the snapped up shadows.

I switch on her music: the heartbeat thump
of the soft rock we've taught her to like.
She feeds on sound.

The bells chime half-past.
The sun has gone and she
tilts from consciousness,

the song and the scream and the jittery light,
this beating wing of body,
this furious little drum.

'Snow'

When she learns the word,
she learns it with a lilt of wonder,
a slow arc of an o

that stays after we've
turned from the window,
after we've left

our boot prints in the garden,
a haphazard snowman
hardening to ice;

stays after the melting,
the last traces of those
lumps on the grass,

stays weeks on, even though
we say it short and straight
and barely ever,

even though by now
she's learning the words
for daffodil and crocus.

The Damage

Slung up, she is an eager tourist,
little limbs dangling from the trunk of me,
head against my too-fast heart.

What's that, what's that, what's that
old oak kneeling on spread limbs,
the billion open doors of its bark.

What's there beneath that high-rise of pine,
its drop zone of nibbled husks
a triumph of collectibles.

She wants to know about the damage:
the wounds where branches were,
the smooth table tops of stumps –

their human angles.
I tell her how the place mends itself,
the small machinery of decay

moving in to mould and remould;
this sodden rug of moss and fungus,
woodlouse, worm and all

the fingertips of the forest
reaching in until eventually
the heartwood gives way;

the giant and tiny bodies
leached into soil. I tell her how
seeds unzip in the mud, grow

down, spreading through the rot.
I tell her there is life, and life,
and she listens, throbbing like wood,

brain branching into all those possible worlds.

* * *

Lichen

       First in, when the dust settles,
when the masons have set down their tools.

         A spattering of paint,
a smudge you'd barely take for life.

Masters of patience, we've formed an alliance
      with the weather.

     Still here, when the rains dry up,
when the soil hardens to rock,

still here when the branches are
            ripped from their trees.

      We spread like cities, make ourselves
part of the stone: see

        that cloudscape silvering your patio,
the signatures graffitied on your outhouse wall.

    Leave us alone
        and we'll colour you a map,

         dress your sculptures in our bling,
run slow riot in the graveyard.

Strike

The children are walking out.
Closing their books,
lessons unlearned.

They gather in the road
like a colony of gannets
perched on a stack,

and above the clamour
of the turning sea,
they lift their beaks,

cry out,
cry out together
for the weight of their wings.

Snake Song

We lifted the lid on your coiled world
and found you in stone-cold sleep,
a shy teen shut up in a curtained room.

Sun ribboned the loose root of you
and we slipped from the skin of ourselves,
as if we'd lifted the lid on a world

we'd almost managed to forget, a relic
of unploughed land, clawed skies.
Harried from your curtained room

you slithered off, dazed, in search
of compost heap or cracked patio,
some new lid for your coiled world

and warm enough for frozen blood.
Another, perhaps, with whom to curl,
shut up in a curtained room, awake

to the noise of footfall and engine,
the warmth of the winter sun, while
we drop the lid on our coiled world,
shut ourselves up in curtained rooms.

Pod

Rain claws at the glass,
the wind plays its chime
like an infant, and we lie
under the hood of the house,
the thought of another
buried like a bulb between us.
We won't sleep now, before
the monitor blares out her quiet
stirring, before she toddles in,
creased and cross,
an armful of bear at her side.
So we lie there
in the rich soil of the night,
listening to the weather's white noise,
raking through our imaginings
until eventually we're not lying
but falling, and the room
is no longer room
but a single seed pod
pouring its cargo earthwards,
and our children grow wild around us,
wind like brambles along borders,
open the red buds of their eyes
on the wreckage of the day.

Spring, 2020

And here is spring, a rash of crocuses
and the river swollen with gathered rain.

Forget-me-nots have hijacked the pots,
dandelions muscle in, poster-paint bright.

Verges buzz with unchecked growth,
spill their residents onto quiet roads,

trees lay waste to the grey, and everywhere
the drip, drip of new, the reckless leap into life.

Spring, and a crowd of bluebells surges,
and the place is pregnant with loss.

Pencil Sketch

As the house shuts up, we write him in,
a pencil sketch of a boy
swaddled in hand-me-downs.

My secret son,
what noise in the night
of your mother's womb?

The growl of the gut,
the heart's weather pounding at your roof,
the pipework of breath and voice

singing through the flesh.
Gone back to our burrows
we draw close,

our rabbit ears pricked for news.
Church bells. Birdsong.
Clap of gunshots in the field.

Prayer

for our scattered loves
the caught and the catching

the kindnesses that stick like burrs
for those we brush against

from a distance, the neighbours
and strangers, those

who would lift us from the blaze
give air, for the science

and sorcery of infection, the body
in all its brokenness, the breath

House on Stilts

That year, I sketched my house on stilts. We're talking
great towering legs, flamingo-thin, a stick family holed up

in a teetering nest of a home, a squiggle of gulls at the window
and a blocky, fishless ocean hundreds of metres down. Access

was an issue: cliff-sheer ladders running the length of an A3 page,
ropes like spider silk dropping from the clouds. There we are

in our creaking ship, the wind crashing like waves underfoot,
the curve of the land lost in the mist, a great canyon of white.

Aubade with Bump

February morning, pocketed in bed,
warmth like a sack of hot breaths,
your hand guides mine to your belly.

And when you twitch, slide my palm
to one side and press my fingers
to your skin, it is so slight it might be

muscle or my own blood, or just
the flutter and kick of imagination
pushing against absence. *There it is again*

– again, did you feel something?

All Well

And now he's here, and all is well,
I find the old tricks gone
and this another game again.

The evening has me jigging out,
the small warm globe of his head
rolling and knocking on my shoulder.

Tiredness grows here:
the uncut grass, the toppled sunflowers,
a blind eye that's life

to ants, drilling holes in the patio,
to willowherb and wild strawberry.
I tap into my phone, *All well.*

He likes the air,
has reached that height from which sleep
is a downward glide,

the pigeons and engines
shushing him along, the swifts
skating currents overhead –

arrows pointing every which way.
Inside, big sister circles
back on the day, its distance

mapped in story and ritual.
Monsters and doctors, doing their thing,
plastic families climbing mountains.

Towers

You ask me what a *real* shame is
– and how blessed

to pretend, how light we are
sat here, stacking. Let's say:

what's left of the music
muffled by wall or worry,

the hollow
where a bridge might go,

the outbreath at the end
of the experiment.

Pick up the bricks, try again.
If I could make it balance,

little architects, I would.

Text Note:

Incompleteness Theorem, p16

This quote is from a letter written by Gödel to his mother in 1961, translated by Yi-Ming Wang, and appears in the book 'A Logical Journey: From Gödel to Philosophy' by Hao Wang (MIT Press, 1997)

www.ingramcontent.com/pod-product-compliance
Ingram Content Group UK Ltd.
Pitfield, Milton Keynes, MK11 3LW, UK
UKHW042004230426
12048UKWH00009B/533